PHILIP J. WATSON

EGYPTIAN PYRAMIDS AND MASTABA TOMBS

OF THE OLD AND MIDDLE KINGDOMS

SHIRE EGYPTOLOGY

Cover illustration
The Step Pyramid of King Djoser at Saqqara.
(Photograph by the author.)

British Library Cataloguing in Publication Data available.

Published by
SHIRE PUBLICATIONS LTD
Cromwell House, Church Street, Princes Risborough,
Aylesbury, Bucks HP17 9AJ, UK

Series Editor: Barbara Adams

ISBN 0 85263 853 1

First published 1987

Set in 11 point Times and printed in Great Britain by
C. I. Thomas & Sons (Haverfordwest) Ltd,
Press Buildings, Merlins Bridge, Haverfordwest, Dyfed.

Contents

4

List of illustrations

Chronology

From Murnane, W. J. *The Penguin Guide to Ancient Egypt*, 1983.

Predynastic and Protodynastic	before 3050 BC		
Early Dynastic or Archaic Period	3050-2686 BC		
		3050-2890	*Dynasty I*
			Narmer
			Aha
			Djer
			Djet
			Den
			Adj-ib
			Semerkhet
			Qa'a
		2890-2686	*Dynasty II*
			Hotepsekhemwy
			Nebre
			Nyneter
			Peribsen
			Khasekhemwy
Old Kingdom	2686-2181 BC		
		2686-2613	*Dynasty III*
		2686-2668	Nebka
		2668-2649	Djoser
		2649-2643	Sekhemkhet
		2643-2637	Khaba
		2637-2613	Huni
		2613-2498	*Dynasty IV*
		2613-2589	Snefru
		2589-2566	Khufu
		2566-2558	Djedefre
		2558-2532	Khaefre
		2532-2504	Menkaure
		2504-2500	Shepseskaf
		2498-2345	*Dynasty V*
		2498-2491	Userkaf
		2491-2477	Sahure
		2477-2467	Neferirkare
		2460-2453	Neferefre
		2453-2422	Niuserre
		2414-2375	Djedkare-Isesi
		2375-2345	Unas
		2345-2181	*Dynasty VI*
		2345-2333	Teti
		2332-2283	Pepi I
		2283-2278	Merenre
		2278-2184	Pepi II
First Intermediate Period	2181-2040 BC		
		2181-2040	Dynasties VII-XI

Middle Kingdom	2040-1782 BC		
		2060-1991	*Dynasty XI*
		2060-2010	Mentuhotep I
		2010-1998	Mentuhotep II
		1997-1991	Mentuhotep III
		1991-1782	*Dynasty XII*
		1991-1962	Amenemhat I
		1971-1928	Sesostris I
		1929-1895	Amenemhat II
		1897-1878	Sesostris II
		1878-1841	Sesostris III
		1842-1797	Amenemhat III
		1798-1786	Amenemhat IV
		1785-1782	Queen Sobeknofru
Second Intermediate Period	1782-1570 BC		Dynasties XIII-XVII
New Kingdom	1570-1070 BC		
		1570-1293	Dynasty XVIII
		1293-1185	Dynasty XIX
		1185-1070	Dynasty XX
Third Intermediate Period	1070-713 BC		Dynasties XXI-XXIV
Late Period	713-332 BC		Dynasties XXV-XXX
Graeco-Roman Period	332 BC-AD 395		Ptolemies and Roman Emperors

1
Introduction

Of all the monuments of ancient Egypt the pyramids are the best known. Indeed the popular conception of the ancient Egyptians is of a people obsessed with death. However, this assumption is unfounded and arises simply from the fact that the vast majority of the remains of ancient Egyptian civilisation are tombs or objects of a funerary nature. Their towns, palaces and houses have for the most part disappeared as they were situated in the fertile valley where land was, and still is, at a premium for the production of food. Tombs on the other hand were built in the cliffs and on the desert where they have remained undisturbed for centuries.

Although it must be admitted that the Egyptians did take elaborate precautions in their funeral arrangements these represent not a morbid preoccupation with death but rather an over-zealous desire for life. They conceived of an afterlife which reflected earthly conditions but in a bigger and better way and so long as they could ensure the survival of their *Ka* or 'essential spirit' in the afterworld they could effectively achieve immortality.

The subject of this volume is the earliest tombs of the historic period, the mastabas and pyramids. In prehistoric or Predynastic times the Egyptians were buried in simple shallow pit graves dug out of the desert sand. From very early on it is apparent that they believed in some form of afterlife as the earliest burials contained pottery and other, more personal possessions. The development of this belief led to the concept of an afterlife which reflected the world of the living and in which the tomb was seen logically as the funerary equivalent of a house. To emphasise this symbolism the simple mound of sand over a grave was soon replaced by a superstructure built at first of mud brick and later of stone. More offerings and paraphernalia of life were included which meant that the tomb had to be enlarged to accommodate storerooms and an offering chapel. The increase in funeral furniture also led to an increased risk of tomb robbing and so blocking portcullis slabs and other security measures were built into tombs.

With the elaboration of funerary beliefs there went a corresponding elaboration of funerary practices and it soon became necessary not only to provide equipment and provisions with the burial itself but to maintain a daily supply of food and drink offerings. In theory these were to be presented by the eldest son of the deceased but in practice, for royal persons and higher nobles, the task was delegated to professional mortuary priests, many tens of whom were attached to the mortuary temples associated with the pyramids. The eldest son would often carry out his duty in person on certain feast days and other special occasions. Land was bound over to the royal mortuary temples and this was cultivated by the staff of priests to ensure a continued supply of food offerings. In addition the priests were, on occasions, exempted from taxes and other services imposed by the central administration. Thus the mortuary priesthood represented a significant factor in the economy.

The pyramids, perhaps the ultimate symbol of ancient Egypt, are a part of this development. Many superstitions and folktales have arisen around them and much nonsense is still written about them under the dubious guise of the 'science' of pyramidology. Such matters are not dealt with in this book and although Egyptology cannot yet offer answers to all the questions about pyramids it is hoped that what follows will at least demonstrate that such answers need not be drawn from the founts of mysticism and romanticism.

2
First and Second Dynasty mastaba tombs

Our knowledge of the tombs of the First Dynasty derives mainly from two large cemeteries, Saqqara near modern Cairo and Abydos in Upper Egypt.

The Saqqara cemetery, the better preserved of the two, was intermittently excavated by W. B. Emery between 1936 and 1956. The First Dynasty tombs form a line running along the north-eastern edge of the Saqqara plateau overlooking the Nile valley. These were amongst the first monumental buildings in Egypt and from their high and at that time otherwise deserted position they would have presented a striking image on the skyline. The tombs are called mastabas after the Arabic word for a low mud-brick bench which they resemble. Their massive form can be divided into three major sections, the excavated substructure, the mud-brick superstructure and various ancillary structures. They conform to a general overall plan though certain architectural developments can be traced, especially towards the end of the dynasty.

The substructure consists of a pit cut into the rock and divided into a series of rooms by mud-brick walls. The rooms normally comprise a larger central burial chamber flanked by four magazines for the more valuable funerary goods. As it was the most important of these rooms the burial chamber was sometimes decorated. One tomb (3504) had wooden pilasters decorated with inlaid goldwork and another was hung with coloured mats. The burial chamber would have contained the body in its wooden coffin, a funerary meal, chests of clothes and furniture. The subterranean magazines contained the rest of the more valuable funerary equipment — jewellery, games, more furniture, further food supplies, tools and weapons. These underground rooms were roofed with wooden beams with planks set across them at right angles. They did not normally have connecting doors and the only means of access was from above. Thus the body and the funerary equipment must have been installed before the chambers were roofed over and possibly even before the superstructure was built. Some mastabas at Saqqara do, however, preserve traces of corridors through the superstructure which would have allowed access after its completion.

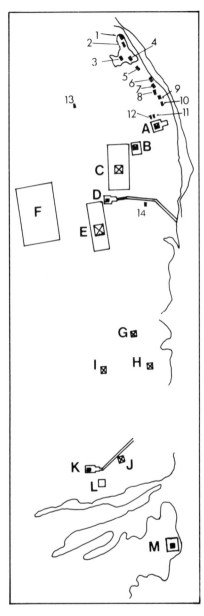

1. (Left) Plan of the Saqqara cemetery. Pyramids and royal tombs: A Teti, B Userkaf, C Djoser, D Unas, E Sekhemkhet, F The Great Enclosure, G Pepi I, H Isesi, I Merenre, J Kakare-ibi, K Pepi II, L Shepseskaf, M Khendjer. Private tombs: 1 3038, 2 3035, 3 Hesire, 4 3357, 5 3471, 6 3503, 7 3504, 8 3505, 9 3506, 10 3507, 11 Kagemni, 12 Mereruka, 13 Ti, 14 Nefer.

2. (Below) Plan of the archaic royal cemetery at Abydos showing the First Dynasty tombs of kings Narmer (B10), Aha (B19), Djer (O), Qa'a (Q), Den (T), Semerkhet (U), Adj-ib (X), Djet (Z), the royal lady Mer-neith (Y) and another member of the royal family (B15), and the Second Dynasty tombs of Peribsen (P) and Khasekhemwy (V).

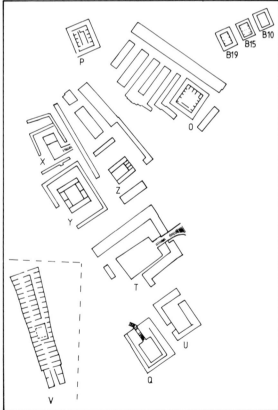

3. The remains of a funerary meal in a tomb at Saqqara as discovered by the excavators. (Courtesy of the Egypt Exploration Society.)

One of the major developments in tomb design during the First Dynasty was the introduction of a stairway providing entry into the burial chamber. This feature was introduced under the reign of king Den around the middle of the dynasty. The stairway started beyond the outer edge of the superstructure so that the latter could be completed before the death of the intended occupant. It descended directly into the burial chamber, invariably from the east (valley) side of the tomb. However, the stairway provided easier access not only for the funeral cortege but also for tomb robbers. Following burial, therefore, a series of stone portcullis slabs, usually three, was lowered down grooves cut in the stair walls.

The superstructure was erected at ground level. It was essentially a mud-brick rectangle usually some 40 to 60 metres

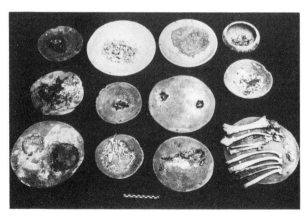

4. Some of the dishes of the funerary meal set out on stone and pottery plates. The menu included ribs of beef, kidneys, pigeon stew, roast quail, triangular and circular loaves, barley porridge, stewed figs and berries. (Courtesy of the Egypt Exploration Society.)

5. The bench built against the panelled facade of tomb 3504 at Saqqara and which was decorated with bulls' heads modelled in clay but having real horns. (Courtesy of the Egypt Exploration Society).

6. Painted decoration on the panelled exterior wall of tomb 3505 at Saqqara imitating the designs of contemporary reed matwork. (Courtesy of the Egypt Exploration Society.)

(130 to 200 feet) long and 15 to 25 metres (50 to 80 feet) wide. Partitioning walls divided the interior into a series of storerooms, twenty to forty-five in number, for storage of the less valuable funerary equipment. In larger tombs each room contained a particular class of object and although all the tombs had been robbed in antiquity enough was left by the plunderers to give us an idea of the original opulence of these burials. For example the magazines of tomb 3035, many of which were completely empty when excavated, still held the remains of 901 pottery vessels, 362 stone vessels, 493 arrows, 305 flint tools, 60 wooden tools, 45 spindle whorls and other miscellaneous items including ivory and textile fragments. In tomb 3504 the robbers had left behind 2500 pottery vessels and 1500 stone jars. The magazines had false floors of clean sand and were roofed with timber. Rubble packing and infill were then used to bring the level of the interior up to that of the outer walls, probably 7 to 8 metres (23 to 26 feet) high. The roofs of the mastabas have in no cases been preserved though it is often conjectured that they would have been rounded with a flat parapet at each end, a shape reflected in wooden coffins of slightly later periods. The exterior faces of the mastabas were

constructed as a series of stepped niches known as panelled facade design, an architectural technique reminiscent of and probably inspired by Mesopotamian religious architecture of the protoliterate period. In addition they were stuccoed and painted with brightly coloured designs imitating the reed matwork which would have been found in the houses and palaces of the time.

Some of the Saqqara tombs (3504, 3506, 3507) had a low brick bench built against the base of the superstructure on all four sides. On top of these benches were set bulls' heads modelled in sun-dried clay but for the horns, which were real. Tomb 3504 was surrounded by an estimated three hundred such heads held in place on the bench by wooden pegs.

In nearly all cases the tombs were surrounded by an enclosure wall and in better examples the resulting corridor between this and the mastaba had a stamped mud floor covered with a thin layer of painted plaster. Servants were buried in subsidiary graves arranged in rows beyond the enclosure wall. These took the form either of individual brick-lined pits roofed with timber or simply of a long trench divided into graves by means of cross walls. In both cases individual superstructures were provided though these were of simple design.

Three tombs (3357, 3503, 3506) had on their north side a brick-clad structure concealing the burial of a wooden (solar) boat intended for the deceased's voyages in the afterlife. Additionally tomb 3357 had a series of model buildings made of solid rubble with a thick mud overlay out of which their architectural detail was cut.

In the tomb of Hor-neith (3507) Emery discovered a rectangular, brick-cased earthen tumulus or flattened mound immediately above the burial chamber and within the body of the superstructure. He also found traces of a similar feature in mastaba 3471 and possibly in 3506. In a later tomb, 3038 from the reign of Adj-ib, the superstructure concealed a second, stepped superstructure which had been enlarged in a rebuilding. As only the

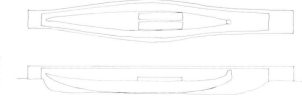

7. Plan and section of the boat burial accompanying tomb 3506 at Saqqara.

lower part of the tomb was preserved it is pure conjecture whether this structure originally continued upwards pyramid-like. Its place in the evolution of the pyramid will be considered later.

Another tomb which contains a feature subsequently more fully developed in the pyramid complex is 3505 from the reign of Qa'a, which is so far unique amongst First Dynasty tombs. It lacks the large number of storerooms in the superstructure and has much simplified and reduced panelling on the west side. More significant, however, is a complex of rooms on the northern end, integrated with the tomb itself by a common enclosure wall. This is to be interpreted as a forerunner to the funerary temple of the later pyramid complexes. In this respect the remains of two-thirds life-size wooden statues, standing with one leg advanced, are particularly significant.

The archaic cemetery at Abydos lies in the area known as Umm el-Qa'ab (mother of pots) and was chiefly excavated by W. M. F. Petrie in 1900 and 1901. The earliest First Dynasty tombs at Abydos, those ascribed to Narmer (B10), Aha (B19) and other members of the royal family (B15, B6, B14), consist simply of an open pit lined with mud brick to form a single burial chamber containing the burial itself and all the funerary equipment. This chamber was roofed with planking resting on wooden beams and posts, over which a mud-brick superstructure was built. None of the superstructures have survived though they are generally thought to have comprised a brick skin over a sand and rubble mound.

Under the succeeding kings Djer (tomb O) and Djet (Z) and the royal lady Mer-neith (Y), the burial chamber was a large wooden construction within the brick-lined pit and the space between it and the sides of the pit was divided into storerooms by means of short cross walls. Large numbers of subsidiary graves were associated with these tombs.

As at Saqqara the tomb of Den (T) saw the introduction of a stairway as a means of access to the burial chamber and this feature was continued in the burials of the later kings Adj-ib (X) and Semerkhet (U). Tomb Q, belonging to the last king of the First Dynasty, Qa'a, shows a further development in that the stairway approached from the north rather than the east. Four rooms at a higher level than the burial chamber opened out from the stairway, two from each side.

The Abydos royal tombs are most notable for the large number of subsidiary burials which accompany them, as many as 317 in the case of Djer's tomb. The practice of burying sacrificed

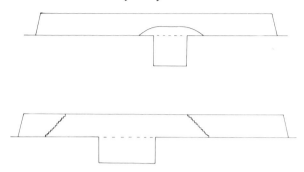

8. *(Above)* Section of tomb 3507 at Saqqara showing the mound-like internal tumulus over the burial shaft; *(below)* section of tomb 3508 with a more substantial stepped structure inside.

servants around the tomb seems to have waned during the course of the First Dynasty and by the end it had ceased.

In addition to the 'tumulus' burials at Umm el-Qa'ab, kings Djer and Djet and Mer-neith also built what have been called 'funerary palaces' in the desert behind the archaic town at Abydos. These consisted of a brick enclosure with panelled walls probably containing magazines and other buildings and certainly surrounded by subsidiary graves. Thus some at least of the First Dynasty kings had two funerary monuments at Abydos — a tumulus tomb on the ancestral burial ground of Umm el-Qa'ab and a palace complex behind the town. At Saqqara these two elements were combined in one structure — a panelled mastaba containing magazines representing the palace, with a brick-covered or stepped tumulus concealed within.

9. The tomb of king Den (tomb T) at Abydos during excavation, showing the stairway leading to the burial chamber. (Courtesy of the Egypt Exploration Society.)

This leads to the vexed question of where the First Dynasty kings were buried, at Saqqara or Abydos? It seemed that the sumptuous tombs at Saqqara must be the royal resting places and that the Abydos tumuli were simply cenotaphs erected because of the traditional religious associations of Abydos as the home of Osiris. However, the realisation that the so-called forts at Abydos probably represent funerary palace complexes altered the balance of the argument and few scholars would now deny that the First Dynasty kings were in fact buried at Abydos. Other factors supporting Abydos as the site of the royal cemetery are the discovery of royal stelae in several of the tombs and the larger number of subsidiary burials there. Many of the Saqqara tombs contain jar sealings bearing the names of high officials and it is perhaps they who are buried there. Furthermore the provision of boat burials at some of the Saqqara mastabas is not necessarily an argument for their being royal.

Several other large tombs of the First Dynasty have survived on sites other than Saqqara and Abydos. Most significant of these from the point of view of tomb development is that of Queen Neith-hotep at Naqada. Like the Saqqara mastabas it has an enclosure wall and palace-facade panelling, but the burial chamber with its four magazines is at ground level, not subterranean. All of these rooms, including the burial chamber, had doorways from the north which had been bricked up and the burial was in a circular depression in the floor. This central suite was surrounded by magazines which had been filled with gravel and sand.

10. Plan of the subterranean chambers of a typical Second Dynasty tomb, that of Ruaben at Saqqara.

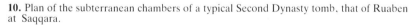
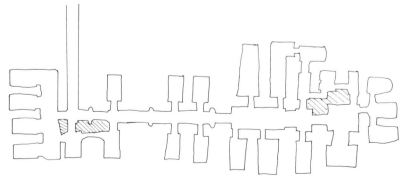

Less is known about the Second Dynasty than the First. The only certain royal tombs are those of Peribsen and Khasekhemwy at Abydos (tombs P and V) with their respective funerary palaces, the Middle Fort and the Shunet el-Zebib. Tomb P of Peribsen is located on the edge of the First Dynasty burials and only the brick-lined substructure remains, consisting of a central burial chamber surrounded by magazines. Khasekhemwy's tomb (V) resembles no other tomb of the period; a northern entrance leads to a complex of thirty-three magazines, a stone-built burial chamber with eight flanking rooms and finally a series of fourteen rooms forming a corridor to a southern entrance.

At Saqqara two complexes of subterranean chambers have been discovered near the pyramid of Unas, one containing jar sealings of Hetepsekhemwy and Nebre and the other jar sealings of Nyneter. It is possible that two of these kings were buried here. The superstructures of neither the Abydos nor the Saqqara tombs have survived. Behind the line of First Dynasty mastabas at Saqqara lie private tombs of the Second Dynasty. These show major changes in design and construction. The subterranean rooms are no longer built within an excavated pit but are tunnelled into the rock. During the early part of the dynasty the substructure consists of a single large chamber divided up into rooms by brick partitions. Tombs of the latter part of the dynasty, however, characteristically have a number of rock-hewn rooms leading off a central corridor. The number of rooms varies from a single burial chamber to large complexes depending on the wealth or status of the occupant. Access was via a staircase normally turning at right angles before entering the burial chamber. Portcullises were still used as a security measure. The superstructures were solid mud-brick or mud-brick over a rubble core and did not contain magazines. The exteriors were plain except for two false door niches on the east side, a larger one at the south end and a smaller one at the north. These were the places where the tomb owner would receive offerings. In some cases the more important southern niche developed into an offering room either within or outside the superstructure.

3
Third Dynasty step pyramids

The problems and uncertainties of the Second Dynasty are left behind by the time of the reign of Djoser (c 2668-2649 BC) in the Third Dynasty. With him begins one of the classical eras of Egyptian civilisation, heralded appropriately enough by his pyramid at Saqqara, the first monumental building constructed entirely of stone. During the Second Dynasty stone, especially granite, had been used in tombs but only for specific parts such as lintels and thresholds. Hitherto buildings had been made almost entirely of mud brick. The new form of royal tomb, a stepped pyramid, must have represented an imposing testimony to the power of the king both at the time and for posterity.

The architect of this pioneering achievement, Imhotep (Greek Imouthes), also attained his due place in history. In his third century BC history of Egypt, the priest Manetho credits Imhotep quite rightly with the invention of building in stone. His reputation as a wise man and healer led to his deification in later times and he was subsequently equated with the Greek Asclepios.

However, this magnificent feat was not achieved lightly nor spontaneously and the Step Pyramid abounds with evidence of several changes in plan and a certain hesitancy about the strength and capabilities of the new building material, incredible as that may seem. This is most noticeable in the small size of block used and the use of engaged rather than free-standing columns.

The Step Pyramid began as a mastaba following Saqqara burial traditions, though even as a mastaba it was unusual in being almost square rather than rectangular. This original structure was built from local stone faced with Tura limestone, a particularly fine-grained, pure white limestone from quarries on the east bank of the river. It was subsequently enlarged by adding a second casing of limestone, 4 metres (13 feet) thick, to all four sides. For some reason this was left slightly lower than the original mastaba, resulting in a small step. A further change in plan extended the east side only by over 8 metres (26 feet) but before this was completed an entirely new design was adopted. All four sides were enlarged to become the bottom stage of a pyramid with four steps. Apparently this version also was not satisfactory as yet further changes were made involving sizable extensions to the north and west faces and elevation to a six-stepped structure.

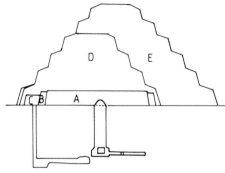

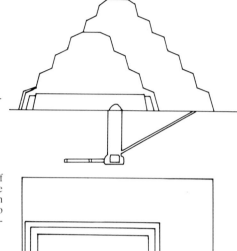

11. (Above and right) Sections and plan of the Step Pyramid of king Djoser: A, the original square mastaba; B, first extension to all four sides; C, second extension to east side only; D, the four-stepped pyramid; E, the final six-stepped pyramid.

12. (Below) View of the Step Pyramid from the south showing the ghost of the earlier structures in the bottom step. (Photograph by the author.)

13. View of the Step Pyramid from the east showing detail of earlier structures. (Photograph by the author.)

Finally a casing of dressed Tura limestone was added.

The development of the substructure was no less complicated. Again following the traditions of earlier mastabas, the burial chamber lay at the bottom of a 27 metres (88 feet) deep shaft excavated out of the bedrock. It was constructed of pink Aswan granite and a hole had been left in one of the roof slabs through which the body would have been lowered. A 3 ton granite block was stored in a room above the burial chamber ready to plug the hole following burial.

The burial chamber was approached by a sloping ramp from the north side of the pyramid. It started at ground level and stopped 12 metres (40 feet) above the bottom of the shaft. However, this entrance was covered over by the last extension of the superstructure and a new approach had to be cut. This also started on the north side but followed a somewhat erratic course until it finally joined up with the original entrance ramp. Midway between this junction and the burial shaft flights of stairs led to a series of underground galleries, some of which are decorated with reliefs and blue glazed tiles.

Beneath the second extension of the pyramid were eleven tombs with deep shafts and tunnels excavated under the pyramid. An alabaster coffin found at the end of one of these tunnels contained the remains of a child. The relationship between these burials and the pyramid is not certain. They are usually thought to be royal and possibly offer an explanation for the second extension, which could be interpreted as a common superstructure for these graves. They are not to be equated with the subsidiary burials of the First Dynasty mastabas.

The pyramid, however, forms only a part of a large complex measuring over 500 by 250 metres (1640 by 820 feet) and surrounded by an enclosure wall 10 metres (33 feet) high. Built from a thick core of local stone and faced with Tura limestone, the wall was panelled in similar fashion to the early mastabas and had fourteen gates irregularly spaced along its perimeter. However, thirteen of these were dummy entrances carved with imitation wooden doors in a closed position. The only true access was through a doorway in the southern end of the east side which led into an entrance colonnade lined with engaged columns and with simulated log roofing carved in stone.

South of the pyramid was a large open court containing a low altar near the south face of the pyramid and two B-shaped objects which perhaps marked out a ceremonial course connected with the royal jubilee. One of the more important ancillary buildings, the south tomb, was situated in a corner of this court. Although it consists of a large mastaba with an offering chapel it is probably the forerunner of the subsidiary pyramid. Its substructure is very similar to that of the Step Pyramid, having a granite burial chamber at the bottom of a vertical shaft with a hole in the roof

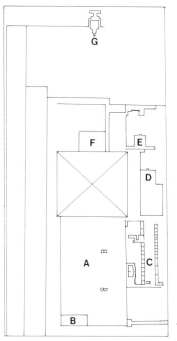

14. (Left) Plan of the Step Pyramid complex: A, south court; B, southern tomb; C, buildings connected with the jubilee festival; D, House of the South; E, House of the North; F, mortuary temple; G, altar in north court.

15. (Below) Section through the Meydum pyramid showing the two stepped versions and the final 'true' pyramid.

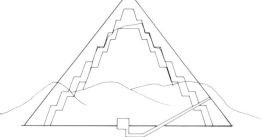

plugged by a granite block. A ramp led to subsidiary galleries decorated with reliefs and glazed blue tiles. The burial chamber was too small to have accommodated a body though the reliefs would indeed suggest that it was intended for Djoser's use. It has been suggested therefore either that the south tomb was a dummy burial for an enacted sacrifice of the king during the jubilee ceremonies or that it was a canopic burial for the internal organs of the body, which were removed before mummification and were often wrapped and buried separately.

The east side of the complex contained several buildings associated with the celebration of the *heb-sed* festival or royal jubilee, which seems to originate from a time when the king was ritually slaughtered after he had reigned for a period to ensure lasting fertility and prosperity of the community. During the *heb-sed* festival the king was magically rejuvenated, thus removing the need actually to kill him. The ceremonies included the ritual running of a course and a re-enactment of the coronation. The jubilee buildings included a rectangular court with dummy chapels of solid masonry, a coronation dais and retiring rooms, the latter constructed to imitate a typical palace or large house. To the north are the so-called 'houses' of the North and South representing the archaic shrines of Lower Egypt (Buto) and Upper Egypt (Hierakonpolis). Each one has a court with engaged columns from which a doorway leads into a cruciform sanctuary containing niches for statues.

The mortuary temple, where the daily offerings to the dead king were made, is exceptional in being on the north side. Next to it was the *serdab,* a room completely sealed off except for two peepholes drilled through the front wall, containing a seated statue of Djoser. The statue served as a resting place for the spirit of the deceased should the mummy be destroyed. Beyond the mortuary temple was a large terrace, at the extreme north end of which were a rock-cut altar and underground storerooms containing cereals and fruit. The west side of the complex is taken up by two long parallel structures of solid masonry of uncertain significance.

Although many of the elements in the Step Pyramid complex appear unprecedented others can be interpreted as part of a developmental sequence. The pyramid itself may represent the inner tumulus of the earlier mastabas and the panelled enclosure wall their outer palace facade. The mortuary temple is the developed form of the offering niche or chapel. The most significant of the new elements is the southern tomb which is the

16. Aerial view of the Meydum pyramid taken in 1930. (Courtesy of the Institute of Archaeology. Crown Copyright reserved.)

prototype for the later subsidiary pyramids. As to the remainder of the buildings one can only conjecture as to whether similar ceremonial structures might have been enclosed within the walls of the First Dynasty funerary palaces at Abydos.

Because of its relatively good state of preservation the Step Pyramid of Djoser tends to stand apart amongst Third Dynasty royal tombs although at least two other similar complexes were begun during the dynasty. The first of these, the Buried Pyramid, lies close to Djoser's complex at Saqqara. It was discovered and excavated by Z. Goneim in 1950 and has been ascribed to king Sekhemkhet on the basis of inscribed jar sealings found nearby. Sekhemkhet reigned for only six years and it is obvious from what remains that his pyramid complex was never completed. However, the essential elements of a seven-stepped pyramid, a panelled enclosure wall and a south tomb comprising a rectangular mastaba over a deep burial shaft have been identified. The substructure of the pyramid was similar to that of Djoser's. The burial chamber was approached down a sloping ramp from the north side which also gave access to 132 underground magazines and to four galleries associated with the burial chamber. If completed this might also have been decorated with blue glazed tiles and reliefs. The south tomb was also similar to Djoser's.

Another, even more badly ruined step pyramid was built at Zawiyet el-'Aryan, between Giza and Saqqara. This, the Layer Pyramid, probably belonged to king Khaba. Only the lowest courses remain of what would have been a six- or seven-stepped pyramid and it is quite clear that it was never finished and also probably never occupied.

A fourth step pyramid complex might be concealed within the so-called Great Enclosure at Saqqara, the rectangular outline of which has been revealed to the west of Sekhemkhet's complex by aerial photographs. This, however, awaits excavation.

The last king of the Third Dynasty, Huni, was probably the king who began construction of the pyramid at Meydum although graffiti indicate that Egyptians in the New Kingdom thought it belonged to Snefru, the first king of the Fourth Dynasty. Again several changes in design can be seen, the earliest determinable form being a seven-stepped pyramid. That this was intended at the time as the final form is apparent from its casing of dressed Tura limestone. However, it was enlarged into an eight-stepped pyramid and again ostensibly completed with a casing of dressed limestone. Finally the steps were filled in and cased to produce a geometrically true pyramid with smooth faces. This final transformation was probably carried out by Snefru, hence the New Kingdom attribution of the monument to his reign. The strongest evidence for this hypothesis lies in the fact that the masonry of the stepped versions is laid in courses sloping in towards the centre of the pyramid as in other Third Dynasty examples. The final layer, however, which filled in the steps, is laid in horizontal courses, the method used in the Fourth Dynasty.

In all three versions access to the interior of the pyramid was via a sloping corridor on the north side. However, presumably in an attempt to fool tomb robbers, the entrance was no longer at ground level but part way up the face of the pyramid, in the first two versions at the level of the first step. The corridor led down through the superstructure and into the underlying rock before levelling off and leading to a vertical shaft, at the top of which was the burial chamber, built partly in the body of the pyramid and partly excavated out of bedrock. It was lined and paved with limestone and had a corbelled roof.

The ancillary structures accompanying the Meydum pyramid were arranged in what would become the standard layout. The enclosure wall, the subsidiary pyramid to the south and the mortuary temple were all descended from earlier models. The latter, however, was now built against the east face rather than the north so that it could be linked to a valley temple by means of a causeway, both of which were new features.

4
The Fourth Dynasty development of the true pyramid

Snefru, the first king of the Fourth Dynasty, was responsible as we have just seen for completing Huni's step pyramid. He also built two pyramids for himself, both at Dahshur, almost 30 miles (48 km) north of Meydum. The northernmost of these, known as the Red Pyramid, is normally regarded as being the earlier and also earlier than the final version of Huni's pyramid. Thus it was probably the first tomb to be completed as a true pyramid. Its most notable feature is the shallow angle of incline of its sides, which is a little over 43 degrees as opposed to the later normal figure of about 52 degrees. The entrance is above ground level in the north face and leads down a sloping passage through the body of the pyramid to three corbelled chambers. The first two are almost identical in size and although the second of them is directly under the apex of the pyramid it is probably the third and largest which was the burial chamber.

The second of Snefru's pyramids at Dahshur was the Bent Pyramid, so called because there is a drastic change in its angle of incline just over half way up its height. The lower portion has an incline of about 54 degrees, the upper portion an incline of 43 degrees, a slope identical to that of the Red Pyramid. This change in angle is usually taken to imply that the pyramid had to be finished somewhat hastily as the lower angle requires less volume of stone to complete the pyramid. There is further support for this theory from the masonry itself, which is less carefully laid in the upper portion. An hypothesis that the angle change was induced by a contemporary collapse of the Meydum pyramid is unlikely as other evidence suggests that the Meydum pyramid did not collapse until after the Eighteenth Dynasty. Its superstructure is the best preserved of any pyramid and it retains more of its original Tura limestone casing than any other. This is doubtless due to the greater cohesion arising from its having been laid not horizontally but in courses sloping in towards the centre as in Third Dynasty pyramids, a method which also had the advantage of requiring less trimming of the casing blocks.

The Bent Pyramid is unique in having two substructures reached by separate entrances. From the north face, the usual entrance position, a sloping corridor descends into bedrock

ending in a corbelled chamber. From the west face a second
entrance, higher than the northern one, leads to another
corbelled chamber higher than, but not directly above, the first.
This second entrance and chamber are built entirely within the
superstructure of the pyramid. Neither chamber contained any
traces of a burial or sarcophagus.

The mortuary temple near the east face of the pyramid was
very simple, comprising essentially an open altar screened by
brick walls. Immediately beyond the enclosure wall on the south
side is a subsidiary pyramid which is unlikely to be a queen's
burial as in later reigns. Rather it probably retains the function of
the Third Dynasty south tomb as a canopic burial or as a dummy
for the jubilee festival. In the latter respect it should be noted that
a fragmentary stela was found nearby depicting the king in jubilee
attire. The causeway, which was unroofed, led to a valley temple
which is now much destroyed although originally of monumental
size and decorated with reliefs.

With the second king of the dynasty, Khufu (better known
under the Greek form of his name, Cheops), pyramid building
reached a climax. His Great Pyramid at Giza was the biggest and
the best of all and, together with the two other pyramids at Giza,
became one of the wonders of the world. The superstructure is
now devoid of its casing and of the capstone but when complete it
would have risen to a towering 146 metres (480 feet). The interior
of the pyramid underwent several changes of design during its
building. From an entrance part way up the north face and
slightly off-centre a sloping corridor and tunnel led down into a

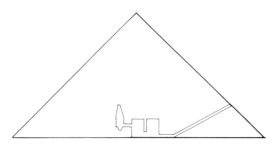

17. Section through the Red, northernmost, Pyramid of Snefru at Dahshur, with a plan of the chambers showing the position of the centre of the pyramid.

18. Sections through the Bent Pyramid of Snefru at Dahshur showing the drastic change in the angle of incline.

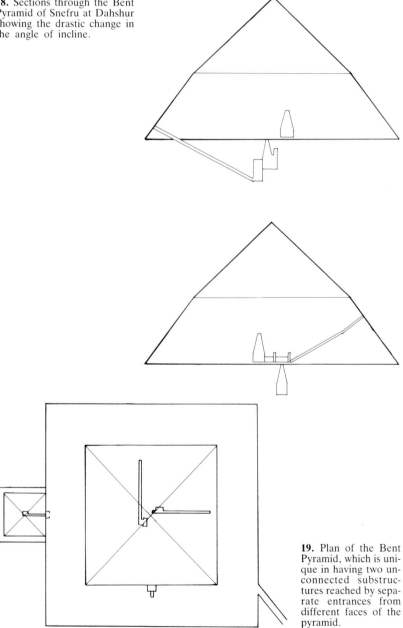

19. Plan of the Bent Pyramid, which is unique in having two unconnected substructures reached by separate entrances from different faces of the pyramid.

20. Plan of the Dahshur pyramid field: A, Sesostris III; B, Snefru's Red Pyramid; C, Amenemhat II; D, Snefru's Bent Pyramid; E, Amenemhat III.

chamber which was never finished because it was decided to construct the burial apartments within the superstructure itself. This necessitated breaching the roof of the descending entrance corridor just above ground level to construct a new ascending corridor. After the burial this aperture was sealed with a block which rendered it indistinguishable from the rest of the corridor roof; it was further protected by three granite plug blocks. From the top of the ascending corridor a horizontal passage was built leading to the so-called Queen's Chamber, approximately beneath the pyramid's apex and intended at the time as the burial chamber. This, too, was abandoned unfinished and the architect returned to the ascending corridor, which was continued in a much enlarged fashion to form the Grand Gallery, a magnificent feat of building. Some 46 metres (150 feet) long and over 8 metres (26 feet) high, it forms a huge corbel vault, the roofing slabs of which are each ingeniously laid at an angle steeper than the slope of the gallery to prevent a build-up of forces on any one point. Beyond a portcullised anteroom the final burial chamber, the King's Chamber, is entered. Built of granite, it has two

21. Simplified plan of the Giza cemetery: A, Great Pyramid of Khufu; B, Pyramid of Khaefre; C, Pyramid of Menkaure; D, the Sphinx; E, workmen's quarter. The main private mastaba fields lie to the east and west of the Great Pyramid.

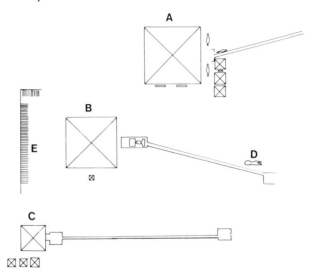

ventilation shafts sloping up through the pyramid to the outside and is unique in having five compartments above the flat ceiling, an innovation which was doubtless intended to minimise any risk of collapse. A passage connected the bottom of the Grand Gallery with the descending corridor, which was used as a way out for the workmen who installed the granite plugs in the ascending passage.

22. Section through the Great Pyramid of Khufu: A, unfinished chamber; B, Queen's Chamber; C, King's Chamber; D, Grand Gallery; E, escape passage.

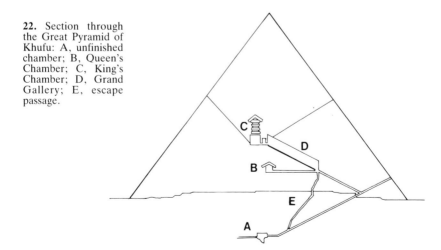

23. View of the Great Pyramid of Khufu at Giza. (Photograph by the author.)

The ancillary structures of Khufu's complex — the enclosure wall, mortuary temple, causeway and valley temple — have virtually disappeared. Five boat pits were provided, one of which contained a dismantled wooden boat 43 metres (141 feet) in length when reconstructed. Although not uncommon in First Dynasty mastabas, boat burials were restricted to royal pyramid complexes for most of the Old Kingdom. The exact function of the boat burials and the significance, if any, of the varying numbers are debated but several plausible hypotheses have been offered based on our knowledge of the funerary and mythological beliefs of the time. For example, one of the boats may have been intended for the funerary journey to Abydos; two more may have been solar barques, one for the day and one for the night; four could have been required for the dead king's journey to the four corners of the sky; one may have been intended for use in the Butite burial ceremonies. To the east of the pyramid and south of the causeway are three subsidiary pyramids for Khufu's queens.

His successor, Djedefre, built a pyramid at Abu Rawash, about 5 miles (8 km) north of Giza. It is unlikely that it was ever finished and little now remains. The substructure is similar to Third Dynasty designs.

The next king, Khaefre (Greek Chephren), returned to Giza for his burial. There he constructed, next to Khufu's, a pyramid complex which represents the standard pattern adopted by subsequent pyramids. Although not as large as the Great Pyramid, it appears bigger, being built on higher ground. Some of the original Tura limestone casing remains near the top as well as some granite casing near the base, although the capstone is missing. It has two entrances, both on the north side, one about 15 metres (50 feet) up the face and the other at ground level cutting through the pavement into bedrock. From the uppermost entrance a sloping corridor descends to just below ground level and then levels off and leads into the burial chamber, the lower part of which is excavated out of the rock whilst the gabled roof is built within the superstructure. The lower entrance descends at a shallower angle, levels out and then rises to join the horizontal section of the upper entrance. An unfinished room leads off the lower entrance corridor and it is possible that this was originally intended as the burial chamber. It is suggested that it was abandoned when it was decided to re-site the pyramid 60 metres (196 feet) further north in order to utilise a natural rock outcrop for the causeway. Both entrance corridors were blocked by granite portcullises.

The ancillary structures of a mortuary temple on the east, separated from the pyramid by a pavement and connected to a valley temple by a roofed causeway, a high enclosure wall, a subsidiary pyramid to the south and boat pits (in this case five) had now become the standard complement and subsequent complexes vary only in size and detail of plan.

The Great Sphinx, which lay alongside Khaefre's valley temple, is associated with his pyramid and perhaps acted as a guardian for it. It was fashioned out of a spur of rock left over from quarrying operations for Khufu's pyramid and is in the shape of a lion couchant with a human head.

Khaefre's immediate successor was an ephemeral king whose name even is not known for certain, perhaps Bauefre. The Unfinished Pyramid at Zawiyet el-'Aryan is normally ascribed to him though there is no firm evidence to date this ruin precisely. The substructure is similar to that of Djedefre although otherwise this badly preserved monument contains little of interest.

The third of the Giza group of pyramids was built by Menkaure (Greek Mykerinus). Its superstructure, at only 66 metres (216 feet) high, is much smaller than the other Giza pyramids. It is cased with Tura limestone except for the lowest sixteen courses,

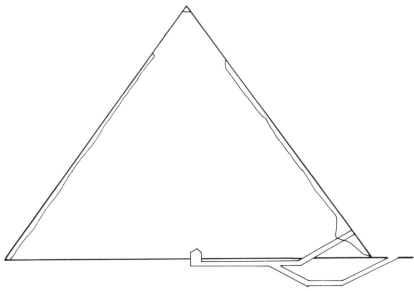

24. Section through the pyramid of Khaefre.

25. View of the Sphinx with the pyramids of Khaefre (right) and Menkaure (left) behind. (Photograph by the author.)

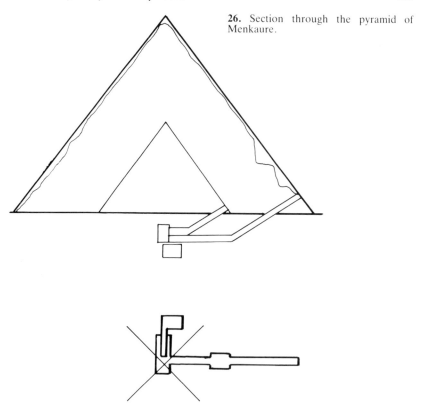

26. Section through the pyramid of Menkaure.

which are finished in red granite. Internally at least one change in design can be discerned. Initially a sloping corridor was tunnelled through the rock to a burial chamber. Subsequently a second corridor was cut below and parallel to the first and the burial chamber was deepened. This alteration is assumed to be due to a desire to enlarge the superstructure whilst retaining the entrance at the same height in the north face. The level section of the second entrance widens at one point to form an anteroom, which is decorated with reliefs. In addition a new burial chamber was added at some stage together with a second room perhaps intended for a canopic burial; certainly it is remarkably similar to a group of supposed canopic shrines in the mortuary temple of Khufu's pyramid. The last burial chamber contained a basalt sarcophagus but this was lost in a shipwreck en route for England.

There is evidence that parts of Menkaure's complex were finished in haste, probably by his son and successor Shepseskaf. For instance, the three subsidiary pyramids to the south were never completed; the mortuary temple was begun in limestone with granite facing but completed in mud brick; the causeway consisted of a brick corridor roofed with timber; the valley temple had stone foundations but the superstructure was built entirely of mud brick.

Shepseskaf himself did not build a pyramid despite completing his father's monument. He constructed the Mastaba el-Fara'un, Pharaoh's Bench, a stone structure in the shape of a giant sarcophagus set on a platform. The vaulted burial chambers were built of granite. Attached to it on the east side was the essential mortuary temple with a causeway leading to a valley temple.

From the beginning of the Fourth Dynasty pyramids were given names and by the Middle Kingdom each part of the pyramid complex had a name of its own. The two pyramids of Snefru, for example, were called the Shining Pyramid and the Southern Shining Pyramid. Those in the Giza group were called the Pyramid Which Is the Horizon (Khufu), the Great Pyramid (Khaefre) and the Divine Pyramid (Menkaure). Note that it is the pyramid of Khufu which we today call the Great Pyramid.

5
Fifth and Sixth Dynasty pyramids

Although at the end of the Fourth Dynasty Shepseskaf had abandoned the pyramid form, the kings of the succeeding two dynasties reverted to it. However, the pyramids of the Fifth and Sixth Dynasties matched neither the size nor the construction of the Giza group. The largest of them, that of Neferirkare at Abusir, was about the same size as that of Menkaure, the smallest of the Giza trio. They were also poorly constructed. The Tura limestone casing concealed cores constructed from small, roughly dressed stones and the majority of them are now little more than heaps of rubble. Although some scholars see this reduction in size and quality as a retrograde step reflecting the waning power of the monarchy and a decline in the economy, it is more likely to indicate a change, if not in philosophy, at least in attitude. The kings of the Fourth Dynasty had tried to overcome death by building tomb complexes whose massive forms and megalithic elements challenged nature itself. Tomb robbers still succeeded in defiling the burials, however, and the kings of the Fifth and Sixth Dynasties put greater faith in the efficacy of narrative reliefs and magical spells to guarantee their survival in the afterlife. Be that as it may, the greatly increased use of low relief decoration on the walls of the mortuary temples, causeways and valley temples more than compensates for the loss of size.

Architecturally the mortuary temple reaches a height of development, adopting the double form of an outer and inner temple. The outer portion lay outside the enclosure wall and contained the entrance hall and a walled open court surrounded by a colonnade. The inner temple occupied the space between the enclosure wall and the east face of the pyramid and invariably contained a room with five statue niches, the sanctuary or offering room and an assortment of storerooms. The plain square or rectangular columns of the Fourth Dynasty funerary temples were replaced by plant-shaped columns with a variety of floral capitals.

Internally the pyramids are very similar in arrangement. The entrance remained on the north side but now started from pavement level, not part way up the face. A sloping corridor descended quite steeply to a horizontal tunnel blocked by portcullis slabs which then led to a rectangular burial chamber. In late Fifth and all Sixth Dynasty pyramids the beginning of the

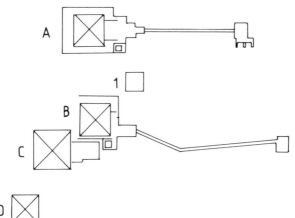

27. Plan of the pyramid field at Abusir; A, Sahure; B, Niuserre; C, Neferirkare; D, Neferefre; 1, tomb of Ptahshepses.

horizontal corridor was widened and heightened to form a small antechamber. The burial apartments consisted of a square vestibule at the end of the entrance corridor with a serdab to the east and the gabled burial chamber to the west.

In all Fifth and Sixth Dynasty pyramids a subsidiary pyramid was built at the south-east corner. The building materials had also become standardised. Local limestone was used for most of the structure, Tura limestone for casing and as a lining for walls to be decorated with reliefs, red Aswan granite for columns, jambs, lintels and so on and black basalt for pavements. In some of the later pyramids alabaster was also introduced to line parts of the burial chamber.

Userkaf, the first king of the Fifth Dynasty, erected his pyramid at Saqqara close to the north-east corner of Djoser's Step Pyramid, which had probably acquired a certain sanctity by this time. Indeed there must have been some such reason for Userkaf's choice of the site as the ground was very uneven, so much so that the mortuary temple had to be built exceptionally against the south face with the subsidiary pyramid on the south-west corner.

The next four kings were buried at Abusir, a little to the north of Saqqara. Sahure's complex surpassed any previous royal tomb in terms of the artistic excellence of its decoration although unfortunately only about one per cent of its reliefs survive; the rest have been used up through the ages for the manufacture of lime. The fragments which survive show scenes of the king's

28. (Above) Aerial view of the Abusir pyramids; that of Sahure is in the foreground. (Courtesy of the Institute of Archaeology. Crown Copyright reserved.)

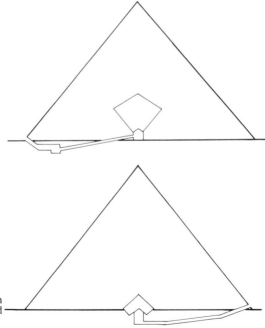

29. (Right) Sections through the pyramids of Sahure and Niuserre.

30. View inside the pyramid of Unas showing a wall covered with Pyramid Texts written in vertical columns of hieroglyphs. (Photograph by the author.)

victory over Asiatics and Libyans, hunting activities and Syro-Palestinian ships, perhaps carrying Lebanese timber. The complex was provided with elaborate drainage systems both for rainwater and for the water used in ritual ceremonies.

His successor, Neferirkare, never finished his complex and its valley temple and causeway were appropriated by Niuserre. This accounts for the change in direction in Niuserre's causeway and probably also for the positioning of his mortuary temple, which is built not centrally but against the southern half of his pyramid's east face.

The later kings of the Fifth and all those of the Sixth Dynasty moved back to Saqqara for their burial ground. Of their pyramids the most significant is that of Unas, the last king of the Fifth Dynasty, situated south of the Step Pyramid. In terms of design and construction it is a typical example and therefore unremarkable although two large boat pits over 44 metres (144 feet) long should be noted south of the causeway. The causeway itself is the best preserved of any and it changed direction twice in order to use various natural features to facilitate its construction. It consists of an embankment with sloping sides on which was built a covered corridor 2.5 metres (8 feet) wide with walls 2 metres (6

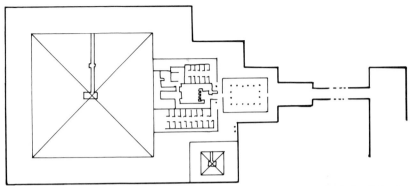

31. Plan of the pyramid complex of Sahure, in which the mortuary temple is within the enclosure wall.

feet 6 inches) thick. Some of the blocks used for it were robbed from Djoser's complex. The walls were decorated with reliefs which would have been brightly painted whilst the flat stone ceiling had stars carved in relief and picked out in gold on a blue ground.

The pyramid of Unas is most notable, however, for containing the earliest known examples of magical spells collectively known as the Pyramid Texts. These are inscribed on the walls of the inner rooms in vertical columns of hieroglyphs which were filled with blue paste. The texts do not form a narrative but are a collection of spells, prayers and hymns arranged in no fixed order. They are found in all the Sixth Dynasty pyramids and some

32. Plan of the pyramid complex of Pepi II, by whose reign the mortuary temple had a markedly bipartite aspect; the enclosure wall bisects the temple, leaving the anterooms outside the wall.

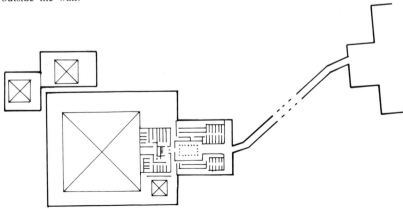

others, although the full repertoire is never found. For example, out of the total of 759 known spells the pyramid of Unas contained only 228.

The central theme of the texts is the rebirth of the king in the afterlife, his ascent to the sky and his induction into the company of gods. In addition there are hymns and prayers as well as various ritual formulae which may have been recited by the priests at certain stages of the funeral ceremony. They were probably collected into a corpus by the priests of the sun god Re at Heliopolis and some undoubtedly go back to the beginnings of Egyptian religious belief. For example, the so-called Cannibal Hymn (spells 273-274) portrays the king as a hunter snaring the gods and eating them in order to acquire their power and properties. A modified version of the Pyramid Texts was inscribed on coffins of the Middle Kingdom (the Coffin Texts) and these, after yet further modification, became the New Kingdom Book of Coming Forth by Day (or Book of the Dead) written on papyrus.

The kings of the Sixth Dynasty all built typical pyramid complexes at Saqqara. Teti's lay to the north-east of the Step Pyramid whilst those of Pepi I, Merenre and Pepi II were close to the Mastaba el-Fara'un of Shepseskaf. Pepi II, who died a centenarian after reigning for ninety-four years, also built pyramids for three of his queens. These all lay outside the enclosure wall of his own pyramid, two to the north-east and one to the south-east. Each was equipped with a complex of its own, even down to miniature subsidiary pyramids.

6
Old Kingdom private mastabas

Whilst the kings of the Old Kingdom were evolving the pyramid tomb the nobles and officials continued to be buried in mastaba tombs. The lower echelons of society were still buried in simple shallow graves excavated in the sand. Before tracing the development of the Old Kingdom private mastaba it will be useful to review the forms of First and Second Dynasty mastaba tombs. It will be remembered from chapter 2 that in the earliest mastabas the substructure consisted of a burial chamber built within a pit and subdivided by mud-brick walls to form magazines. During the First Dynasty a stairway was introduced to provide access to the burial suite, which by the end of the Second Dynasty could comprise a complex of rock-cut rooms leading off a central corridor. The superstructures of First Dynasty mastabas had niched palace-facade exterior walls painted in bright checks and other patterns to imitate reed matwork. This gave way in the Second Dynasty to sides which were completely plain except for two niches in the east face, a larger one at the southern end and a smaller one at the north. The multicoloured patterns of First Dynasty tombs were replaced by superstructures simply painted white.

In the Third Dynasty funerary architecture diverged into an exclusively royal type, the pyramid, and a non-royal type which represents the continuing development of the mastaba. Initially Third Dynasty mastabas were very similar to those of the Second Dynasty, consisting of a complex of underground passages topped by a plain mastaba with two offering niches. During the dynasty, however, the number of subterranean rooms was reduced until by the Fourth Dynasty it was usual to have just a single large burial chamber. This remained the dominant type throughout the Old Kingdom. The Second Dynasty stairway approach was retained at first but soon gave way to a combined stairway and vertical shaft and then to a shaft alone, although many intermediate combinations can be adduced to illustrate the gradual manner in which the shaft tomb came to prominence. In early examples the burial chamber was tunnelled into the south face of the shaft but from the Fourth Dynasty onwards it was always on the west side. The superstructures showed a similar development in that they were initially plain with two offering niches. During the Third Dynasty there was a revival of the

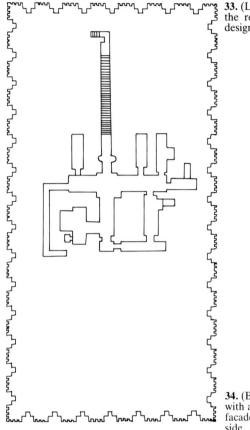

33. (Left) Plan of mastaba T at Giza; note the revival of the niched palace-facade design in Third Dynasty tombs.

34. (Below) Plan of tomb 3070 at Saqqara with a typical corridor chapel and niched facade on one side, the east or valley side, of the tomb only.

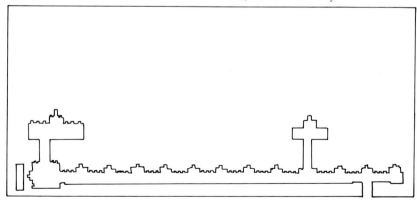

niched palace facade in some mastabas, occasionally on all sides of the tomb (such as Giza mastaba T) but usually only on the side nearest the Nile valley (for example Saqqara 2405 [Hesire], 3070) and sometimes in a simplified version. Third Dynasty mastabas continued to be built either of solid mud brick or of mud-brick casing with a rubble filling. However, stone was increasingly used for lintels, jambs, thresholds and other specific architectural elements, culminating in the stone mastabas of the Fourth Dynasty at Giza with their fine limestone casing over a solid core of local stone. Henceforth stone was the standard building material for richer burials though lower ranks had to remain content with brick.

The most important development to take place in mastaba architecture was the evolution of the area set aside for making offerings to the deceased. The southern, more important, offering niche with its simple brick exterior chapel tended to become more complex, especially in larger tombs. Third Dynasty brick mastabas often had a so-called corridor chapel in which the entire eastern, or valley, side of the tomb was walled off to form a long narrow corridor leading to the southern niche. The offering niche itself gradually assumed the form of a room within the body of the mastaba, often cruciform in shape. In the stone mastabas of the Fifth and Sixth Dynasties the trend was towards an increasing number of subsidiary rooms all built within the superstructure, which effectively became a large mortuary chapel. There are many variations of plan amongst such mastabas and although the essential elements remain the same there was no adherence to a standard layout. Not all tombs adopted complex chapels and many retained solid superstructures with a one-room chapel.

This development reflects to a certain extent that seen in the royal tombs, where the tendency was for the superstructure (the pyramid) and the burial apartments to become simpler whilst more emphasis was placed on the complexity of the mortuary temple. The decoration of royal and private tombs follows a parallel development. Initially simple reliefs depicting the deceased king are found, but with the Fifth Dynasty emphasis was given to the magical spells of the Pyramid Texts and the ability of reliefs depicting scenes from life to act as substitutes for the sustenance of the spirit of the deceased should his relatives or mortuary priests become remiss in their provision of offerings. As with royal tombs there is little decoration in Third and Fourth Dynasty private mastabas, although some superb examples of

35. (Right) Carved wooden panel from the tomb of Hesire at Saq-qara (Courtesy of Peter A. Clayton.)

36. (Below) Painting of geese from a Fourth Dynasty tomb at Mey-dum (Courtesy of Peter A. Clayton.)

early Egyptian art have come from such tombs, in particular the carved wooden panels from the tomb of Hesire at Saqqara and the magnificent painted geese from a Fourth Dynasty mastaba at Meydum. With the Fifth and Sixth Dynasties raised relief decoration carved on the stone walls of the chapel becomes common. The reliefs are striking enough to the modern eye yet originally they would have been painted in bright colours, adding still more to their impact. They depict a variety of subjects but the most important scenes, which are invariably found in the main offering room containing the false door stela, show the deceased seated before a table piled high with offerings with a full tabulated list of provisions given nearby. The deceased is normally shown in company with his wife and children and occasionally the family pet animal is also included. In the larger tombs files of bearers are shown bringing in further offerings. The remaining rooms are carved with scenes which reflect, and in which we can glimpse, the everyday life of the people of the Nile valley over four thousand years ago. Commonest are scenes depicting all aspects of agriculture and gardening, with fishing and bird trapping in the marshes or hunting in the desert as favourite secondary themes. In addition there are vignettes drawn from the work of butchers, bakers, vintners, brewers, metalworkers, carpenters, stone masons and sculptors, boat-

37. A typical funerary scene showing a man and his wife seated at a table of offerings. (Courtesy of Durham University Oriental Museum.)

38. Relief decoration in the tomb of Nefer at Saqqara showing vintners at work. (Photograph by the author.)

builders, jewellers and so on. There are scenes of scribes at work recording, of the deceased relaxing at a banquet and being entertained by musicians, dancers and acrobats. Ultimately there are funeral scenes. In short, few aspects of ancient life cannot be found depicted somewhere on the walls of an Egyptian tomb.

The major elements of the mortuary chapel were the false door stela and the altar, both placed in the main offering room. The false door was carved in a design imitating the reed doors of Predynastic houses. It was usually inscribed with the names and titles of the deceased and his family tree as well as an offering formula. Ideally the false door was placed as directly above the burial chamber as possible, as the spirit of the dead occupant was thought to be able to pass through it in order to partake of the offerings which were provided either in fact on the altar or magically by the reliefs and inscriptions on the chapel walls. The serdab was another feature normally found in the more important mastabas (see page 22).

The private mastabas of Old Kingdom officials tended to be constructed in well ordered cemeteries around the pyramids of the kings whom they served. It is possible here to give only a brief survey of these mastaba fields, as they are usually termed. The largest concentration of Third Dynasty mastabas is at Saqqara, to the north of the Step Pyramid and behind, that is west of, the First Dynasty mastabas. The best known of them is the tomb of Hesire, an official under Djoser. His solid mud-brick mastaba had a combined stairway and shaft approach to a complex of

39. Section through a typical Fourth Dynasty mastaba.

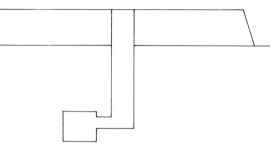

subterranean rooms. It had a corridor chapel on the east side, the interior of which had scenes of offerings painted on a white ground and carved wooden panels in the doorway. The exterior of the mastaba was panelled on the east side only.

Tombs of the Fourth Dynasty tend to be concentrated in the cemeteries of Giza and Meydum. The main mastaba fields at Giza lie to the east and west of the Great Pyramid. The nucleus of these cemeteries consists of stone mastabas contemporary with the reign of Khufu, many of them built by royal masons and presented to officials and priests as rewards for long or valued service. They tended to conform to a regular pattern and were originally set out in neat rows but later tombs were built in amongst them so that the layout now appears rather haphazard. The standard Fourth Dynasty Giza mastaba had a stone superstructure with gently sloping sides. A shaft which was filled in after burial penetrated the superstructure and bedrock,

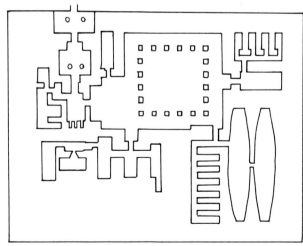

40. Plan of the mastaba of Ptahshepses at Abusir.

terminating in a small tunnelled burial chamber. They were the first private tombs in Egypt to be built entirely of stone. At Meydum the Fourth Dynasty mastabas arranged around the pyramids continued to be constructed of mud brick. Many of them have a peculiar feature in that they possess cruciform chapels which have been bricked over and replaced by a simple niche.

As already noted, larger Fifth and Sixth Dynasty mastabas are remarkable for their complex, magnificently decorated chapels and lack of uniform plan. At Saqqara there is an important group of such tombs to the north of the Unas causeway, some of which (such as the tomb of Nefer) were buried during its construction and were therefore better preserved. Other notable tombs lie to the north of Teti's pyramid (such as Mereruka and Kagemni) and near the Apis galleries (tomb of Ti). As well as the main offering room and the serdab the Saqqara tombs often have a pillared room and the tomb of Kagemni had two boat pits on the roof. At Giza the Fifth and Sixth Dynasty mastabas are simpler in plan but no less well decorated. Particularly notable are the tombs of Qar and Idu in the east cemetery and in the west the mastaba numbered G2000, which, although totally undecorated, is so massive that it must have been the resting place of a very high official. Finally mention should be made of the dense mastaba field to the north of Niuserre's pyramid at Abusir. This contains an example of an Old Kingdom mastaba at the height of its development in which the funerary chapel is so extensive that it occupies virtually the whole of the superstructure. The inner apartments of this tomb, which belongs to Ptahshepses, have five elements. The main part of the chapel has an antechamber, a three-niched offering room and side chambers. From it access is gained to a porticoed hall off which leads a group of rooms connected with the burial, a set of chambers including two boat-shaped rooms and a further set of offering rooms.

Mastaba tombs tended to be a specifically Memphite feature. Further south they appear only where the ground is suitable, for example at Abydos.

7
Middle Kingdom pyramids

Following the collapse of the Old Kingdom at the end of the Sixth Dynasty, due to economic disorders and increasing appropriation of power by the nobility, Egypt entered a period of instability with fragmented government under feeble dynasties for almost a century and a half. A few pyramids are known from this First Intermediate Period but because of the relative weakness of their royal builders they are of no great size and little importance.

The kings of the Eleventh Dynasty built tombs on the west bank of Thebes, their home town. The earliest kings, Intef I and II, sited their tombs at Dra Abu el-Naga. Both were similar in plan, having a rectangular court with a tomb tunnelled into the rock face behind. A ledge was cut out of the rock above the burial chamber and a small brick pyramid, about 15 metres (60 feet) square, was built on this. It obviously represented only a token gesture to the traditions of royal funerary architecture. The tomb of Intef III has not yet been located although it is usually assumed that it would have been nearby and similar.

In the mid Eleventh Dynasty Mentuhotep I, who is normally regarded as being the first king of the Middle Kingdom, selected a bay in the cliffs at Deir el-Bahri for the site of his burial. Here he constructed what was one of the most innovative examples of funerary architecture in Egyptian history, now badly preserved and sadly overshadowed by the Eighteenth Dynasty funerary temple of Queen Hatshepsut, whose design owes much to Mentuhotep's monument. It is probably best summarised as being a mortuary temple with integral tomb. It had an associated valley temple, with which it was connected by an unroofed causeway. The mortuary temple itself had a large outer courtyard enclosed by a wall built from small limestone blocks and planted with a garden of tamarisks and sycamore figs. From it a ramp led to an upper terrace. To either side of the ramp was a colonnade. The upper terrace held a large columned hall, on three sides of which were colonnades. In the centre there was a solid structure long thought to be the base of a pyramid but now suspected to have been more mastaba-shaped. At the back of the pillared hall were six shrines with vertical shafts leading to tombs for six ladies, wives and daughters of the king. Subsequently, the temple was extended further into the cliff, adding an inner colonnaded court and a hypostyle hall containing eighty octagonal columns

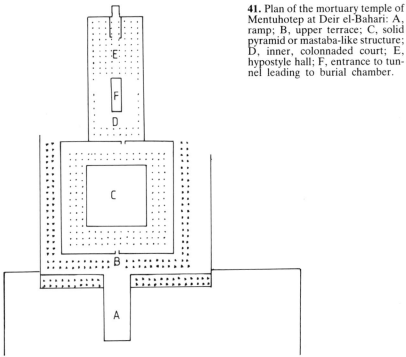

41. Plan of the mortuary temple of Mentuhotep at Deir el-Bahari: A, ramp; B, upper terrace; C, solid pyramid or mastaba-like structure; D, inner, colonnaded court; E, hypostyle hall; F, entrance to tunnel leading to burial chamber.

and the sanctuary to the royal cult.

Provision for the burial was originally a shaft from the outer courtyard leading to a set of rooms beneath the solid structure in the pillared hall. These were never finished though they may later have served the purpose of a cenotaph. Following the extension of the temple a new burial suite was provided. Access was through a concealed entrance in the inner, colonnaded court from which a corridor led down beneath the hypostyle hall deep into the cliff to a granite-lined burial chamber. Mentuhotep II began construction of a similar but smaller monument south of Deir el-Bahri but it was never finished.

Amenemhat I, founder of the Twelfth Dynasty, transferred the capital from Thebes to a site between Memphis and the Fayum. He also reverted to essentially Memphite burial traditions, building a pyramid complex at Lisht similar to those of the Old Kingdom pharaohs. The pyramid itself was built on a terrace and the inner core contained many decorated limestone blocks robbed from Old Kingdom tombs at Dahshur, Saqqara and Giza.

The mortuary temple on the east was similarly built largely with reused blocks and was also set on a terrace which was lower than that of the pyramid. West of the pyramid, but beyond the enclosure wall, there was a row of tombs belonging to members of the royal family. As in the late Old Kingdom the entrance to the subterranean rooms was at ground level on the north side. A corridor lined with granite and blocked with granite plugs led to the burial chamber, which has never been fully investigated.

Amenemhat's successor, Sesostris I, also built his pyramid at Lisht. Although it is remarkably similar to Sixth Dynasty complexes it contains the first of the Twelfth Dynasty innovations in pyramid architecture. The superstructure was not built up in a solid mass but rather a framework was constructed of walls running from the centre to each of the corners and to the middle of all four sides. This formed eight compartments which were further divided by cross walls and then filled in with rough blocks of limestone set in sand. When complete the superstructure was cased with Tura limestone. The entrance to the sloping corridor leading to the burial chamber was on the north side under the pavement of a small offering chapel.

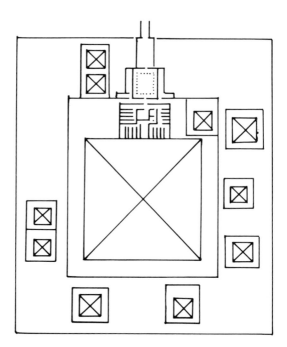

42. Plan of the pyramid complex of Sesostris I at Lisht. The smaller diagram *(below)* shows the arrangement of the skeletal walls within the pyramid.

The ancillary structures in this complex are also strongly reminiscent of Sixth Dynasty examples, especially the bipartite mortuary temple. The valley temple, causeway, subsidiary pyramid on the south-east corner and the enclosure wall all follow Sixth Dynasty traditions. Beyond the inner wall were nine much smaller pyramids, arranged apparently indiscriminately around all four sides, for the burial of royal ladies. Despite having their own mini-chapels and mortuary temples these 'harem' pyramids lacked the detail found in those of Pepi II's queens and did not have miniature subsidiary pyramids. The entire complex was enclosed within an outer brick enclosure wall.

Amenemhat II built the White Pyramid at Dahshur but it was not until his successor, Sesostris II, that further innovations were introduced. The superstructure of his pyramid at Lahun comprises a natural knoll of rock some 12 metres (40 feet) high on which the now standard skeleton of cross walls was built. The lower courses of the wall were of stone, the upper ones brick. The compartments were filled with mud brick, not stone, and henceforth all Middle Kingdom pyramids were built of brick apart from their casing of limestone. The second new feature was obviously introduced in an attempt to combat tomb robbers. The religious significance of a northern entrance was abandoned and access was via a shaft, off-centre, on the south side of the pyramid. From the bottom of the shaft a passage led upwards through several small chambers and a right-angled turn to the burial chamber containing a granite sarcophagus. Other passages almost forming a square led off the main passage and back to one end of the sarcophagus, though their purpose is somewhat puzzling. On the north-east corner there was a subsidiary pyramid and the east and south sides and part of the west had been planted with trees, the pits for which were discovered beyond the brick enclosure wall.

Both Sesostris III and Amenemhat III built pyramids at Dahshur and used brick for their superstructures, concealed their entrances (to the west and east respectively) and sited the burial chamber amidst a maze of passages and false rooms. Amenemhat III had a second brick-built pyramid at Hawara, of which the mortuary temple was the 'labyrinth' of classical authors. Again elaborate precautions had been taken to foil tomb robbers. The entrance in the western half of the south face led down a flight of steps to an antechamber. Beyond this was a short passage with a concealed trap door in the roof giving access to a chamber off which ran a long blind passage northwards and a genuine passage

43. (Right) Plan of Sesostris II's pyramid showing the cross-walls used in its construction.

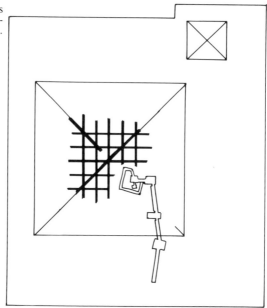

44. (Below) View of the pyramid of Sesostris II at Lahun. (Courtesy of Peter A. Clayton.)

45. (Right) Plan of the Hawara pyramid of Amenemhat III showing the antechambers (a), the blind northern passage (b), the ceiling traps (c), the two false shafts (d) and the burial chamber (e).

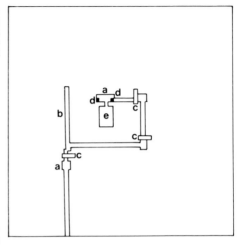

46. (Below) Section through the massive vault over the burial chamber in Amenemhat III's pyramid at Hawara.

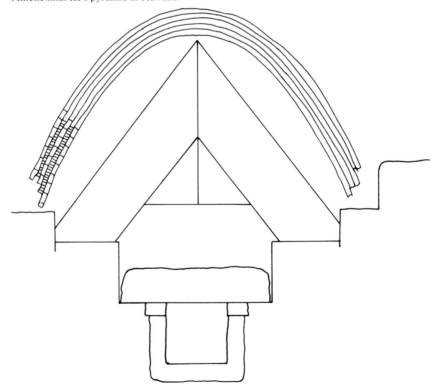

which, after two right-angled turns and two further ceiling traps, led to a second antechamber. This was provided with two false shafts sunk into the stone at each end and a false wall as well as the true entrance to the burial chamber. This was through a trench in the floor which had been carefully paved over. The burial chamber must have been constructed before the super-structure as it comprised a single massive piece of quartzite, hollowed out and lowered down a shaft in the bedrock. Its weight has been estimated at over 100 tons. Above it are two relieving chambers, with flat and pointed roofs respectively, and the weight of the pyramid above is distributed further by means of a massive brick arch.

Two pyramids at Mazghuneh, south of Dahshur, resemble the Hawara pyramid and it has been suggested that these belong to Amenemhat IV and Queen Sobeknefru. Effectively these are the last pyramids.

Following the Middle Kingdom a few pyramids are known from the Second Intermediate Period, the most notable of which is that of Khendjer at Saqqara. All are similar to the late Middle Kingdom examples. The kings of the Seventeenth Dynasty built tombs at Thebes topped with small brick pyramids and some private tombs, especially those of the Nineteenth Dynasty at Deir el-Medina, were also surmounted by miniature pyramidal structures.

Finally there was a late revival of the pyramid form by the Twenty-fifth 'Ethiopian' Dynasty of Nubian pharaohs in their cemetery at Napata in the Sudan.

8
Materials and methods of tomb construction

The Egyptians of the Old and Middle Kingdoms had relatively restricted technological means. They had no lifting devices in the modern sense, used no wheeled vehicles and had limited mathematical knowledge. Nevertheless the accuracy of alignment, orientation and measurement of the Great Pyramid of Khufu is impressive by any standards and the near perfect jointing of its outer blocks would be the envy of many craftsmen.

The material of the earliest mud-brick mastabas was abundant. The bricks were made from Nile mud mixed with chopped straw to give it greater cohesion and to prevent cracking when it dried. They were shaped in rectangular wooden moulds and left to dry in the sun. During building the bricks were set in mud mortar.

Obviously the pyramids presented much greater problems and the hesitancy with which stone was first used has been seen in the Step Pyramid. One of the first stages in pyramid construction was levelling the site, or at least the outer perimeter of it as in some cases natural prominences were incorporated into the core. This could have been achieved quite easily by building a wall around the site and filling it with water. A level surface could then be obtained by cutting down to an equal depth all over. The area would have been measured out using knotted ropes or perhaps by counting revolutions of a wheel or drum. Accurate orientation could have been achieved without the use of a compass by marking the rising and setting positions of a star on an artificial horizon and then bisecting the angle between them to give true north. This would have involved observing the star from, say, the centre of a circular walled enclosure, using a siting device which the Egyptians are known to have possessed.

Such surveying methods are, however, purely hypothetical, though eminently plausible, as the Egyptian texts are silent on such matters. Much more is known about the techniques used to quarry, dress and smooth the stone. The tools employed consisted of dolerite hammers or pounders, copper chisels struck with wooden mallets and wedges driven into grooves in the stone to separate it from the rock face. The majority of the stone for the core of a pyramid was quarried locally and therefore had to be transported relatively short distances. The finer Tura limestone

47. View of the first pylon in the temple of Amun at Karnak showing the remains of a building ramp. Note that the face of the pylon is not decorated, thus explaining why the ramp had not been dismantled in antiquity. (Photograph by the author.)

for the casing and reliefs and granite from the quarries at Aswan were brought as close to the site as possible on barges. By transporting such blocks during the inundation season they could be floated to within a mile of the site at most and in some cases as near as 250 yards (230 metres). On land, blocks were strapped on to wooden sledges and dragged along causeways set with timbers which were lubricated to reduce friction.

There is no evidence that the Egyptians had any sort of lifting device at this period and they were certainly ignorant of the principle of the pulley. In order to raise blocks to the necessary level sloping ramps of brick and rubble were built at right-angles to one or more faces of the pyramid and the blocks could be dragged up these. As the pyramid grew in height so the ramp was both raised and lengthened in order to maintain the same gradient, usually 1 in 10 or 1 in 12. In step pyramids it is possible that ramps were built parallel with the sides, rising one step at a time and running helter-skelter-wise around the pyramid. Once up the ramp blocks were slid into position on a thin layer of fine mortar.

Herodotus records that 100,000 men were used in the construction of the Great Pyramid and that the work took twenty years.

This is almost certainly an exaggeration. Estimates based on study of the remains of what are presumed to be workmen's quarters to the west of the pyramid of Khaefre at Giza suggest that some four to five thousand men were permanently employed on the pyramid site itself. In addition to these one must add the workers in the quarries at Tura and Aswan. It has already been seen that the blocks from these quarries would have been transported during the inundation, a period when the majority of the population, who were farmers, would have been unable to work. It is likely, therefore, that a system similar to that of the corvée existed whereby the otherwise idle labour was employed on pyramid construction, doubtless receiving thereby a welcome supplement to their agrarian income. After completion the outer casing of the pyramid would have been dressed smooth from the top downwards as the ramps were dismantled.

The relief decoration in the mortuary temples and the private mastabas was executed by a variety of craftsmen. The slabs were first dressed smooth by stoneworkers. Next an artist inked out the main design, the outline of which was carved by a stone mason. The artist returned and added the secondary features and any detail, which were then engraved by the mason before he removed the background. The latter operation was achieved by pounding, not chiselling or chipping, which might have caused the stone to flake and so mar the design. After polishing with a quartz sand abrasive the reliefs were painted using simple mineral paints. Copper ores such as azurite and malachite were used for blues and greens, ochre, iron oxide and other iron salts for yellows, reds and browns, chalk for white and some form of carbon, probably soot, for black. They were applied with a frayed reed brush dipped in an aqueous solution of gum.

By the skilful and patient application of these simple methods and materials the Egyptians constructed their monuments of eternity, the largest of which has so far stood for over four and a half thousand years and still elicits the awe of those who look upon it, causing the name of its builder, Khufu, to be remembered in the mouths of men, thereby ensuring him the immortality which he sought.

9
Museums to visit

The following museums have Egyptology collections. Intending visitors are advised to find out opening times before making a special journey.

United Kingdom
Ashmolean Museum of Art and Archaeology, Beaumont Street, Oxford OX1 2PH. Telephone: Oxford (0865) 512651.

Birmingham Museum and Art Gallery, Chamberlain Square, Birmingham B3 3DH. Telephone: 021-235 2834.

Bolton Museum and Art Gallery, Le Mans Crescent, Bolton, Lancashire BL1 1SA. Telephone: Bolton (0204) 22311 extension 379.

British Museum, Great Russell Street, London WC1B 3DG. Telephone: 01-636 1555 or 1558.

City of Bristol Museum and Art Gallery, Queens Road, Bristol, Avon BS8 1RL. Telephone: Bristol (0272) 299771.

Durham University Oriental Museum, Elvet Hill, Durham DH1 3TH. Telephone: Durham (0385) 66711.

Fitzwilliam Museum, Trumpington Street, Cambridge CB2 1RB. Telephone: Cambridge (0223) 69501.

Manchester Museum, The University of Manchester, Oxford Road, Manchester M13 9PL. Telephone: 061-273 3333.

National Museums and Galleries on Merseyside, William Brown Street, Liverpool L3 8EN. Telephone: 051-207 0001 or 5451.

Petrie Museum of Egyptian Archaeology, University College London, Gower Street, London WC1E 6BT. Telephone: 01-387 7050 extension 2884.

Royal Museums of Scotland, Chambers Street, Edinburgh EH1 1JF. Telephone: 031-225 7534.

Sheffield City Museum, Weston Park, Sheffield S10 2TP. Telephone: Sheffield (0742) 27226.

Australia
National Gallery of Victoria, 180 St Kilda Road, Melbourne, Victoria 3004.

Austria
Museum of the History of Art: Egyptian and Oriental Collection, Burgring 5, 1010 Vienna 1.

Belgium
Royal Museum of Art and History, Avenue J. F. Kennedy, 1040 Brussels.

Denmark
New Carlesberg Gallery, Dantes Plads, 1550 Copenhagen.

Egypt
Aswan Museum, Aswan.
Egyptian Antiquities Museum, Tahrir Square, Cairo.
Greco-Roman Museum, Museum Street 5, Alexandria.
Luxor Museum, Luxor.

France
Museums of the Louvre, Palais du Louvre, 75003 Paris.

Italy
Egyptian Museum, Palazzo dell'Accademia della Scienze, Via Accademia della Scienze 6, Turin.
Egyptian Museum, Vatican City, Rome.

Netherlands
National Museum of Antiquities, Rapenburg 28, 2311 EW Leiden, Zuid Holland.

Sweden
Museum of Mediterranean and Near Eastern Antiquities, Jarntorget 84, Stockholm.

United States of America
Metropolitan Museum of Art, 5th Avenue at 82nd Street, New York, NY 10028.
Smithsonian Institution, 1000 Jefferson Drive, SW, Washington DC 20560.
University of Chicago Oriental Institute Museum, 1155 East 58th Street, Chicago, Illinois 60637.

West Germany
Egyptian Museum, Schlossstrasse 70, 1000 Berlin 19.

10
Further reading

The following bibliography lists some of the more popular books which are generally available either through booksellers or from libraries. Readers wishing to consult more detailed or specialist works should refer to the extensive bibliography given by Edwards, although these can usually be found only in larger reference libraries.

Edwards, I. E. S. *The Pyramids of Egypt.* Penguin, 1970.
Emery, W. B. *Archaic Egypt.* Penguin, 1982.
Faulkner, R. O. F. *The Egyptian Pyramid Texts.* Oxford University Press, 1969.
Goneim, M. Z. *The Buried Pyramid.* Longman, 1956.
Jenkins, N. *The Boat Beneath the Pyramid.* Thames and Hudson, 1974.
Lauer, J. P. *Saqqara: The Royal Cemetery of Memphis.* Thames and Hudson, 1976.
Spencer, A. J. *Death in Ancient Egypt.* Penguin, 1982.

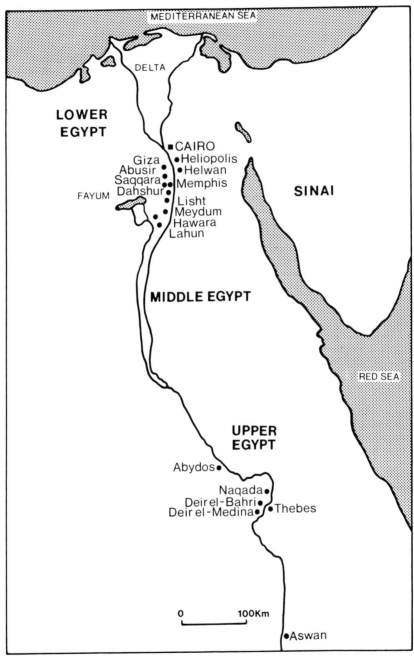

48. Map of ancient Egypt showing places mentioned in the text. (Drawn by D. R. Darton.)

Index

Page numbers in italic refer to illustrations